The Secret Land

Patrick Sheils

A Publication of The Poetry Box®

Editing & Book Design by Shawn Aveningo Sanders.
Cover Design by Robert R. Sanders.

ISBN: 978-1-948461-20-7
Printed in the United States of America.

Acknowledgments:
I would like to thank Shawn Aveningo Sanders and Robert R. Sanders at The Poetry Box for their hard work and dedication with this project. I would also like to thank the professors in the English department at SUNY Old Westbury for their help throughout the years.

Published by The Poetry Box®, 2019
Beaverton, Oregon
ThePoetryBox.com

To Carol

Contents

One Room in Copenhagen

Where I can close my eyes in a foreign world
on a world that disappeared

Home, where the heart dies.
Lies.
What a cynic I've become!

Home is a room in Copenhagen
where you can close your eyes in a foreign world
on a world that disappeared.

The clouds open to a starless sky
far beyond the illusory figment
of childhood imaginations
intentional daydreams
innocent enough to turn vinegar sweet.

Can I cultivate this batch of parts
and assemble a long chain polymer
wide enough to bridge one room in Copenhagen
to the world that disappeared
and turn on the lights
of sleeping dreams on the verge of spring.

I Am Rachel

You can have your whimsical delusions,
she said to me.

In a world where the hovering dead form clouds of communal
    technology
that reverse the tides of the Long Island Sound
you can have your whimsical delusions

I am Rachel.

It never stops, as you can tell.
How so much white can fall from so much gray…

Can you dig me a road of reinforced steel,
so that I may cross this oasis and save the world
from the jagged edges of razor snowflakes
fiberglass winds that bleed our lungs dry
and drown us in forgotten poisons.

Whispers speak of a summit overlooking the spherical dwellings
of the last vestiges

of heart and soul.

You must sacrifice me with the killing device
you keep concealed from hesitant eyes
that cannot look away from the fragmented remnants
of head on collisions.

My eyes must close on the sorrow of the elders
whose tears have frozen in sculptured mosaics
choking the life out of this land.

I must walk the path of regeneration
and bring color to drab oils
that cough the parasitic phlegm
killing the grass before it grows.

I must stand upon the cemetery of the world
and open my wrists

so that slumber may cease
and the offspring of my cells may mate
with the dormant buds of potential
who thirst for existence
in ways only the blind can understand.

And as I fall to my knees
closing the book on the old ways
I will gasp out my last words
laughing at the gods while they cover their ears
only to hear

I am Rachel.

Once

There was, once. What was the query? Where is the once
that you so often recall with instantaneous reflex? Or are we
        referring
to somatization
of inadequate negative responses
to a wish unfulfilled.

To harken to the once as if it wears a red suit
and throws its weighty rear end down the chimney.

Well, you're at least half correct.

The algae covered shore rocks which break the façade
of the reflected self
in the impact is the once.
Here, there, everywhere?

Nowhere.

Kick the sardine can a few feet up the coast,
let the next guy deal with this.
Maybe, just maybe he wears the protective equipment
of metallic cylinders lubricated in 32-weight.

Maybe he can defend himself from the monster
that has devoured
the children in the day school
where I received a gold star
for unparalleled participation.

Six Chambers

Pick up the pistol. Let us dance the waltz of false starts
and dead ends.
Let's look to the skylights of falling debris
for we know the truths that connect to ashen memories.

Kodak never-never lands whose hulls fill with water
and descend to the unmeasured depths
of an amber ocean.

Cock the hammer. Let us fox trot through a scrap yard
of rebuilt trannies and choked out carburetors
where guppies disperse in dirt water potholes
and greasy boots spread the pollution of way-back-when
over a landscape of rust and kerosene.

Pull the trigger. Let us embrace the rebirth of the world
where the sun will poke his head out of the horizon
like so many startled housewives
alone in the shower.

Can we taste the cinnamon as our tongues gauge which way the
        wind blows?
Never so magical a time to be alive.
We can see the shooting star fairies
as we follow their trail of glitter blood to the top of
Mount Olympus.

Toast to the gods of debauchery.
To cabernet waterfalls and supple breasts
in countless abundance!

Empty out the chamber! Let us consume
for an eternal eternity
that travels in both directions.

Let us have it all!

The hillside towns that rumble beneath commodity mudslides
and the cityscapes that sway back and forth
off the fumes of our pilgrimage!

Salud, chindon to campfires of familial traits
that manifest in universes unobserved
waiting to be plucked
from the garden of idyllic virgin concepts.
Let us empty our pens of red ink
onto transfixed margins that govern our world,
for emergent creativity may flourish
amongst even the most rigid of right angles.

Let our emptied-out shells rest.

Let our emptied-out shells rest.

Altered Palettes

Are your tastes refined?
Maybe it would be more appropriate to ask
if they *have* refined
from a palette that only tastes backwards
indulging in a 24 oz cyanide capsule cooked medium rare
with a side of arsenic
and a glass of 18 year old antifreeze neat.

This hotel of the tasteless cynics
has reached maximum occupancy.
Paintings of the Rhynie Chert fossil beds
the only prized Picasso's that hang
on a wall painted in the blood of banana war
casualties.
The bell for room service has rung
delivered by the trickster of Babel
whose wrinkles flow downstream
and collect in puddles from the leaky ceiling.

The lights stay on while the rest of the world has turned in for the
    night.
Dreams manifest into realized realities
within the confines of this
torrent
whose mechanism refines chaos
into ordered paranoia
where so many horrors are produced.

The fire exits to a stairwell
composed of turning lawn mower blades
have been sealed shut, ensuring
the assumed occupants
that this is the home they were destined for.

Through a tiny crack in the ceiling
of the top floor luxury suite
a curious entity forces its way to the floor.
Different in kind.
In composition.

One cannot say how a palette can be changed
After so many lifetimes of absinthe and hydrogen peroxide
yet the curious nature
of a fearless entity taking the shape
of both entrance and exit
may be a start.

There are so many flavors to indulge in
depending on which side of the entity you reside.

Listen...

Listen.

It's Your Turn to Pick Up the Tab

In moments, the sensory stimulation carries us.
It brings us back to the table. We relish the opportunities.
We enjoy them at once. We smile upon the gifts
offered to the temple
that we ingest in kind.

In moments, we are taken away resolutely from metaphysics.
We celebrate the temple
accepting its faults as we accommodate the structural limitations
and bolster its architectural integrity
as we see fit.

Many times, these on-site decisions may be misguided
yet we listen to the voice who maintains the atrium
who in turn listens to the vegetation
that dictate their desires.

In moments, we cannot embrace dramas yet to be read.
We wear the celebratory blinders
of thoroughbreds at Belmont
running in circles
on kicked up mud and Kentucky bluegrass.

In moments, we cannot see the faces of the crowd
only hear the collective groan
that turns individuality
into a deadening white noise.

The sound of silence?
No, for in the moment we do not accept contradictions
only deterministic impulses
weighed on the scale of tar and feathers.

Impulses?
Surely such arguments can only be made
from the safe distance
of the other side of a story arc.
Where snow covered mountain tops
melt at the behest of a cosmic grandfather clock.

Such irony, that in moments we cannot see
in moments.
That the foundational structure
where the metaphysical joy of the moments is given value
lives so far away
that the moment becomes a part of microwave background
    radiation.
Or maybe they *are* just pigeon droppings.

Such sadness
that the false comforts of nostalgia are destined
for a perverted brand of
Contradictory Buddhism
where all moments of self are sacrificed
for an overarching sense of self
that feeds off the broken backs of our hard work.

How I'd love to meet that overlord.
Give him the bill
and say

"This one's on you, you cheap prick."

It's Snowing in Delaware

They were stuck on a glass road of lottery balls
percolating in a life-sized coffee machine.
You could smell the burnt beans ten exits
North. South.
East. West.

In the name of the
Father. Son.
Holy. Spirit.

Looks like an accident up ahead.
The leather upholstery is screaming at his lot in life
slaughtered for the comfort
of equally sized blonde and blue-eyed cows.
I think his cousin is digesting right now
commiserating through gaseous expulsions
about how neither of them ever had a chance.

It's raining so hard.
Someone up there must have just gotten a proper spanking.
The water catches hang in a delicate balance
perpendicular to a gated community
of farm dwelling ne'er-do-wells.
It's been said they bury their young next to their baby teeth
but no one has conducted a proper investigation.

I think they call it Tiny Town.

Blue stone buildings of barbed wire windows
frozen in dry ice speckle the debacle.
This coffee needs some milk.

Ah, that's right!
It's snowing in Delaware!
If only we could get there.
How do we get there?

Follow the road, of course.

Well, how do we do that?

[. . .]

You wait for the right numbers to pop up.

Right, of course.
Well, what do we do if the numbers never come out a winner?

You sit here ten exits back
next to Tiny Town
until it's all over.

But it's snowing in Delaware!

Hey, what do you want from me?

Deceptive Knights

There is no difference in kind between
the invisible wind
and the air of death.

A cot in a prison cell of pre-determined dimensions
anchored in the resolve of
raging fires
transformed into dead forests
and underwater civilizations
thriving in the memory of a child
who has yet to taste the smoke.

Forever indebted to the invisible wind
that comforts the withered bones
of the fossilized primate
with an ace up his sleeve
and a holstered revolver by his side.

The deceptive invisible, so welcome a distraction
that we equate so easily with the
humidified air of death
that turns dry at High Noon
when the earth turns its back on the sun
into the empty darkness of space
where the moon has fallen out of its rotation.

The way of the wind
and the weight of the air
are the Black and White Knights
that clash in the shadows
while we swallow the pills of amnesia
convincing ourselves
they are one and the same.

These Premises are Under Surveillance

This may be the case, sometimes I wonder
if the inner reality removed from sights and sounds
could ever be purveyed
by premises under surveillance.

One day they may throw a parade
another a life sentence.

Celebrate the creativity of an artist
or curse the twisted thoughts
of a disgraced narcissist
who so readily indulges from the well
of corporeal satisfaction.

I hold in my hand three tokens of chance
to be played in slot machines
in a casino burial ground
where the players ghost dance on the filtered wishes
of peace
hundreds of years past their Sell-By date.

I pray for the tokens to correspond to
7-7-7
so that I may forget about the ghost dance
and rent the luxury suite filled with
Terry cloth robes
and five star meals at the push of a button.

If these premises are under surveillance
could they hear the thoughts
before they materialize on the paper
rendering this exercise
as useless as a pin-less grenade?

If these premises are under surveillance
what does that say about the words
that dump themselves onto the page?

Only that the author may be the one
who set up the surveillance system
so that the walls of the premises
may be taken down
and his gradual agoraphobia
may be relegated to the margins of
superfluous Friday night plans
and midnight snacks.

Secret Land

The timeless architecture of Tudor dwellings.
Time-less
Less-time

Take me to this secret land and its impenetrable police barricade.

Let me ride on the wind of Quetzalcoatl
to a secret land void of doors and ceilings
where the potential of timeless architecture resides
in the complete absence of architectural structures.

As it orbits around my heart
as my heart orbits around its perfect symmetrical beauty.
In the end, perhaps
I will penetrate this secret land
inhabited by the Baroque compositions of
masters of the discipline.

No.

The potentiality of Baroque compositions
masters of the discipline manifested
whilst twiddling my opposable thumbs
from the comforts of an Ikea sectional.

Communicative properties filtered through the eons
of carboniferous death matches
and desert dwelling miscreants
cooked under the sweltering heat
of the god of the Prisoner and Philosopher.
Even this god forever subservient to the secret land.

As we expand through the drama
of thieves and prophets
decrying decrees of their enemies
in tribal pursuit of the gods of the now
propped up by the secret land

I so long to understand
yet know I never will.

rorriM

We haven't spoken in a while.

I remember a time not long ago, hell it could have been yesterday
when you were but a dispensable arbiter
of potential courtship.
How badly I wish to take a blade
to that yard of dead grass collecting on the upside-down hill
that anchors your asymmetry.

You're a bastard.
A chameleon born of Cordyceps spores
sprinkled about a dirt path
with upside down coordinates.
You talk until your words become the howl
of a spotted terrier
who still pisses on the newspapers
in a 40,000 dollar renovated kitchen.
The smell has seeped through the floors.

Your foreign tongue has been sharpened
I can tell.
I have yet to decipher your words
but I feel the sharp cut of your forged blade
you keep sheathed in the petrified xylem cells
of a long deceased douglas-fir.
God, you're a prick.

Of course, I cannot dialogue with you.
There are no eardrums, no heart nor compassion.
Only
the unending tape loop of a communist sadist
whose sexual proclivities begin and end
end and begin
with hearing his own voice
that only we can hear.
You're a self-fornicating sex doll.

How I envy your ability of mastered ambivalence.
The fact that only I bear the consequences of your indifference
the conflated receptors of your murderous decrees

delivered in perfect pitch
neatly spread across the eternal uniformity
of a bass and treble clef.

I'm tired.
Allow me my rest, if only momentarily.
You have all night to write another play.
The roses thrown on the stage of last night's production
are still wet.
I shall clean them up for you before I go to sleep
so that you'll have a clean work station in the morning.

I love you.

Antiquities Kitchen

Gradual progress is made
in the kitchen of antiquity
filled with devices that feign function.
The carcasses of the backyard
Dangle in solemnity.

Do we pray for these wonders
bridging the elders to their young
where shared communion at the table
evaporates the limit of knowledge.

In the welcoming embrace of antiquities kitchen
the hidden promises of transcendence
whisper in children's voices
a sound that cannot be heard until the table is cleared.

Questioning why it is such
that trophies so desired are possessed
all along
cloaked in shadows behind willow trees
that smile at the stove in antiquities kitchen.

Desire so gripping that limbs atrophy
stuck in a snowbank
in an upside down gravitational pull
while their bitter thirst rips the skin
off their feet
towards the water well under the smiling willow

whose leaves, only in falling
communicate the prayers of the living
as if to say look around later
for now you can only see in ways you do not yet understand
as it breathes in the aromatic life wafting from antiquities kitchen.

As languages change so shall you
while sourced in the unchanging reservoir
of antiquities kitchen.

Art Gallery

This is the best in the world
at least that's what they say.
Monoliths of iconography
transformative behind a fisheye lens.

Everything is a mathematical structure from above.

Count the blessings of uncultivated promise
destined for an eternity within the rectangle.
How many rectangular eternities we see in this world!
Where does the rectangle live?
That is the art gallery for me.

Corners, where the homeless sleep
and the gutter rats pilfer for scraps.
Corners, where the street sweepers fail to reach
And water run-off accumulates ever more bacteria.
Corners hold the painting together
so as not to drift off
expanding into nothingness
until a cold death separates every last particle
and the self is gone.

Bless these corners in the gallery
deemed unworthy of monoliths.
Corners are everything.

Can You Trust?

Would you take him at his word
if fixations of anticipatory anxiety
crumbled at the sight
of mindful distractions between friends?

The comrades of yesterday's worrying
wear not the black leather gloves of 32 degrees
rather the dentured white smile
of an old set of bleeding gums
that drool at the sight of dangling worms
on a hemlock fishing rod carved countless wars ago.

Hear the prosperity gospel of cold calling salesmen
as their greased hands slip out of your grip
when they pat you on the back with
post-it notes.

"We got a live one here!"

Go ahead.
Try getting the hook out of your mouth as it fuses
to the wet skin of your cheek
that dries up after so many turned calendar pages
of sermons shouted from the rooftops
of roofless skyscrapers.

Find treasure in the foundation, flooding with water.
Loose electrical wires that dangle
next to vents
blowing the hot air of standardized deductions of
personhood
kicked back by the lonely cries of reductionist sorrows
that carry the self through the rising tide to Hades.

That cloaked mannequin versed in the ways of deception
waiting for the water
to lick those wires
and fry the whole place
without ever lighting a match.

[...]

You cannot trust the ghosts, for their words are
but petrified ink blots
in a notebook that if time forgot
so must you.

You cannot trust the ghosts.

Bedtime Stories

Her hands frost bitten, wrinkled and dark
hurt so profoundly.
Never could she imagine the pain of catching fire
until her hands were this cold.

The factory on the corner of home
anticipates 100,000 more assemblies tomorrow
of dollar signs contained within the closed windows
of frost bitten hands.
Only in a place like this
is tomorrow guaranteed.

The crack of a leather belt can be heard in the office upstairs.
Gentleman Boss Man
keeps his cigars in a humidifier.
Table stains on a coaster-less hunk of treated wood
home to the imprints of swollen diabetic ankles
that cannot say no to instincts
tugging on a pecker
or cooking in a pan.

Fifteen feet separate
frostbite and Cuban smoke
so much more expensive than American smoke
while American frostbitten hands
are so much more expensive than
their Cuban counterparts.

Hey, it is as it is for a reason.
No?

No.
It is as it is because Gentleman Boss Man says it is.

Go ahead, try and tell him otherwise.
See how far that will get you.

The poetic images that mind's eye sees
live next to the signals of pain directed

towards the extremities that cook the steak
on Gentleman Boss Mans dinner table.

There are sons, daughters
oblivious to the conditions in this cold box.
They see with their eyes only the smile
that forces itself through a tired face
in desperate need of a pillow
a blanket
and a hug.

Endless.

A Simple Circle

Take this ring
engraved in the dust particles
of evolutions long and sordid tale
that binds each atom
bereft of identity
and carves out a haven
for the weary travelers that lost their way.

Take this ring designed so long ago
forged on the shore of ocean smacked sand
where masochists return
to the beasts stomach
that digests the salt
and purifies the magnetic consciousness
that joins two lines into an engraved ring.

Let this union rest on your finger
so that the extension
becomes the whole.
Read into the variants what you will
knowing that in simplicity
the complex is understood.

This union needs no polish
for life is defined in the grime of the world
that so illuminates the clean
as the veil
of the genuine bride.

Can we look out onto a cliff so tall
over a lake within steps?
Hoping that the thin line between
here and there
protect this ring from the deep swimming serpents
glowing in conditions
that would flatten the fiercest warriors on our battlefields.

Don't you understand that a scarf around a neck can strangle
and that a battery is finite?

Bring forth the confidence of cave carved witnesses
that dance in the absence of light
and sleep under the roof of stars
that hold heaven in place.

Walk on your hands
the ring will propel you
to see in an upside down world
what the bats in the pines have known all along.

That which you create cannot be uncreated.

Use this ring and remember
that it lives only when forged
to you.
To
you.

Follow the Trail of Sand

I hold in my pocket an unusual amount of sand.
I'm not exactly sure how it got there
and I feel its weight, don't get me wrong.
But I don't mind.

I hear the voices of my tired beloved
worn out from the sharp angles of a geometric world.
I take the small pin from my lapel
and jab a tiny hole in my pocket
dropping a little sand on the ground.

I follow the voices around our little ecosystem
leaving a small trail behind me.
I take on the circumstances of the unfavorable
accumulating more weathered rocks
that fall to the ground in uniform regularity.

At night I dance alone on a rooftop terrace
for the tired beloved
so that the wind of my movement may create
a gentle breeze that brushes upon their face in the morning.

At sun rise I paint the canvases
of blue skies and puffy clouds
with blue crayons and drug store cotton balls.

I follow the voices of my tired beloved
leaving a trail of sand as I continue on.

My hair shows the signs of winter and I feel the weight
in my pocket
begin to lighten.

I must call my beloved. Come one!
Come all! There is a sight to behold!

Put the worries and doubts you carry around with you
in your sore backs
and heavy bags away
for they have no purpose anymore.

[…]

Feel the breeze on your face
hear the ocean waves that crash
upon this beach I have made for you.

Live here now, let this be home.
You deserve it so.
I am not worthy for you to share this with.
I ask only that you enjoy it in my absence
and think not of me again
for the rest of your days.

And when you grow weary
and bored
follow the trail of sand
for there are more paradises waiting for you.

Be tired no more.

.44 on a Dash Outside the Lemon Lounge

Cadillac Deville
aerodynamic as a brick.
Luxurious buttoned seats fart with every movement
of spaghetti filled rear ends contained
in silk dungarees.
.44 on a dash.

In trying to find where the motivation lies
for decisions with life on the line
I can only ask...
Is it up here or in here?
If one could crack open the round casing of wet matter
and probe with a microscope
could they find the source?

What does it take to snuff out a life
in the subjective eyes of blind men
who smell only blood
and taste only money.

Can we throw their vices on the grill
and barbeque them black?

Can we spit on the unjust
and kick them while they're down?

Does it even matter if they feel the pain?

An entity intimately knowable
And curiously misunderstood.

I'm curious of the fascination with paradoxes
illusions
and phantoms of an opera
with a black and white crowd.

Lift off the mask of pretension
and throw it down the garbage chute

that rests next to the noisy neighbor
whose rat weed creeps into the vents
and tickles your nose in moments of tranquility.

Why is it that muffled voices outside of comprehension
tantalize
yet the audible declaratives
of breathing distance
turn off the receptors of communication
and bring us back into contemplative paradoxes?

Tell me!

Where could one think to find any such answers
other than in the notebooks of scoundrels
that smack their lips and drool on the wedding vows
of discarded gods?
How sad a statement
that only through the most rotten of them all
can we learn how rotten we all can be.

Cast them away to the meat grinder.
Let's eat the sausage of idols and swindlers
and raid their dressers
and the cash shoved under a mattress
and use it to buy back the lives
of the ones fucked over
by incomprehensible derelicts
who live only in violence.

She Only Read on Sunny Days

She told me a long time ago
to find her in the book by the windowsill
atop a red ottoman
and a pair of black glasses.

I remember the way her head would tilt
and rest on her hand
the way it would
if she were talking to a dog.

But the creatures whose lives were contingent
on the sun in the windowsill
were so much greater than dogs.

If books are best saved for a rainy day
then why would she only read in that chair
when the living room was painted gold?

When she was sad
she listened to sad songs.

I never understood why she wouldn't try
and cheer herself up with happy tunes during the down times.

But living has a way of clarifying
childhood curiosities
and revealing truths
not interesting enough to speak about for too long.

Sometimes you just have to ride it out
and sometimes sitting alone in silence
on a sad and rainy day
is better than having that crap
ruin a good book.

She has long since passed
and I seldom look at her photographs
for I know I can always see her
in her most radiant glow
in the book by the windowsill.

The Divided Doctor

Cold sweats greet him at four thirty in the morning
freezing under a ceiling fan
set at the highest speed
for particle acceleration uncovering
the hidden structure of the
divided doctor.

There are people under the stairs
in the loft of the decorated man
seeking revenge for the deliverer
of words unforgettable
that remain imprinted in the soul
long after crossing over to the nice neighborhood
up the block.

Why did he sacrifice so many years?
Work his hands into retractable claws
whose purpose has so perverted
his youthful intentions.

No one dreams of batting .250

How does one prepare for delivering such sorrow
horror
?

He only wishes to help. He leaves
milk and cookies for the people under the stairs
reparations for a failure at the table
while four bars of a diminished
piano scale play
on an invisible instrument housed under the light
of a telephone pole outside.

Nothing
Nothing
Nothing
can prepare you for the instant where the face
of the friend changes.

Visualization of a healthy flower permanently bloomless
in the fraction of time it took
for their soul mate to hitch a taxi ride
to the nice neighborhood up the block.

He's too tired. The people under the stairs grow in strength.
They far outweigh the earthly inhabitants lucky enough
to survive on the table
under the retractable claw
of the most celebrated surgeon in a 1000-mile radius.

If only anyone knew
of the people that haunt him
in times when sweat freezes
and the subatomic structure of the divided doctor
is shown to be made
of the rotten flowers he planted in the backyard.

Liars

You don't actually believe all of that, do you?

Count the breaths in between words
only to find a giant sign that reads
fuck you, sucker
spray-painted backwards.

Count the yellow teeth in a rotten cesspool
of ingestion
where saliva washes away the sins of excesses
with anticipatory salience.

We know full well the alchemy of the deceptive.
They speak in Grade-A tongues
displayed in shiny glass cases
at the butcher shop downtown.

They wear magnetic emojis on the lapels
over their heart and hang
bagels
on their hard-ons
with handshakes like factory flounders
whose scales have flaked off
in a mound of stench high enough
to tongue kiss the ozone layer.

I'd rather be in Montreal.

Wafting Around

A man plays a harmonica outside of an abandoned warehouse
      downtown.
The bricks in the street uneven
cracked
wavy.
White caps speckled under a fading street light
you can hear beyond the music as they crash
upon a sidewalk shore.
Far beyond that, a faint sound wafts in the wind.

A group gathered around a barrel fire sing the songs
of incinerated moths
who couldn't help but dive in head first
to their orgasmic death.
The flames discard their aging telomeres with declining rapidity.
The harmony follows suit.
Far beyond that, a faint sound wafts in the wind.

An old man walks out of a jazz club
as the froth that sits atop an improvised concoction
overflows into the street.
He is at peace with himself
drawn to something near to his heart
that echoes in the distance.

They all meet somewhere in the middle
where the faint sound escapes
like smoke blown against the wall
reminding them
that no matter which way the compass points
there will always be a faint sound that wafts in the wind.

Under a Purple Bandana

It sits atop the hairless frame of the eternal warrior.
Her blade has begun to rust
yet she can't help but smile

Stained with the oxygenated blood of past conquests
that take on the hardened form of homes painted so far in the past

you can see the chasm between that time and this time
and fight to keep the chasm alive.

In the distance a triumphant horn can be heard
riding on a breeze of optimism.

The warrior falls face first in the mud.
She inhales the liquid dirt into her lungs
choking on the centipedes
that spontaneously reproduce
in microscopic pockets of air.

She coughs up blood. Her casing has grown weak. It
cracks
creaks
bre-aks.

The repairs are beginning to cost more than the car is worth.

If

worth is married to function
in a utilitarian world she feels alone.

Acid rain begins to singe holes on her shell.

She vomits the mud back where it came from
and wipes off her mouth underneath a purple bandana.
The rusted sword stabs the robust soil that sleeps under the
    battlefield
and helps her to stand.

Even in a maelstrom of enemy soldiers
firing squads
snipers and saboteurs
she navigates her way to the triumphant horn
riding on a breeze of optimism.

For she knows that she cannot allow herself to be stuck
in a game of musical chairs
with room only for the standing.
She realizes that her heart and the horn share the same source.
Waving her rusted sword in the air she rushes
across the crimson plane
smiling under a defiant purple bandana.

The Realized Sacrifice

Could it be that for the first time
part time lovers in a Stevie Wonder song
are the steam for a train headed west
to a gold rush of toothless
sociopaths
and egregious bartenders
that sell poisoned whiskey by the ounce?

Tone-deaf, their parochialism
practiced in the inner sanctum of
courteous troubadours.
Their love affair with penniless wanderers
a blanket of wolf skin
that hides the burning infants of Carthage
that cry in the smoke of spewing volcanoes
forming mountains beyond mountains
where sick eagles are chained to the nest
and can only cry to the blind forces
of the parochial tone-deaf.

Please, wipe the schmutz off your face
as it is plain to see there are hardly any slices
of the peach pie left to consume
that was intended to cool in the evening breeze.

Or are you in fact the bear of the woods
swatting at the beautiful mermaids
in a river of milk?

Don't lie to us, for it is so
unbecoming for even the most deceptive
of impulsive creatures.

If I could buy you a ticket to the
far place
where they speak of a woman named Rachel
you would see that your trickery has been conquered.
Your comrades have turned to dust
and blow in the wind of the Sacrifice.

How have you not received the memo?

And there you go.

I know tomorrows desserts
will be enjoyed
and the tone-deaf shall hear the choir
that smile in unison.
Whose collective breaths
have blown the contaminated waters
out of the dam
so that the pilots of the red cross
may safely land their planes
and we may all feast again.

About the Author

Patrick Sheils is an ISA Certified Arborist and Arboricultural Consultant. He is currently studying English as a graduate student at Tiffin University. He holds a Bachelor of Arts degree in English from SUNY College at Old Westbury and a Career Diploma in Landscape Design from Ashworth College. He is a Certified Environmental Specialist with the International Association of Continuing Education and Training and holds additional certifications with the New York State Department of Environmental Conservation.

Patrick is a professional member of both the Cornell Cooperative Extension and New York State Arborists. He was inducted into the Pi Lambda Theta International Honor Society in 2007. His poetry and short stories have appeared in the Spring 2018 issue of *Harmonia Creative Writing Journal* and the Winter 2018 issue of *Aberration Labyrinth*. He lives in Oyster Bay, New York.

About The Poetry Box®

The Poetry Box® was founded by Shawn Aveningo Sanders & Robert R. Sanders, who wholeheartedly believe that every day spent with the people you love, doing what you love, is a moment in life worth cherishing. Their boutique press celebrates the talents of their fellow artisans and writers through professional book design and publishing of individual collections, as well as their flagship literary journal, *The Poeming Pigeon*.

Feel free to visit the online bookstore (thePoetryBox.com), where you'll find more titles including:

Keeping It Weird: Poems & Stories of Portland, Oregon

The Way a Woman Knows by Carolyn Martin

Giving Ground by Lynn M. Knapp

Broadfork Farm by Tricia Knoll

The Poeming Pigeon: A Literary Journal of Poetry

Psyche's Scroll by Karla Linn Merrifield

November Quilt by Penelope Scambly Schott

An Eyeful of Hennepin Neon by Rheanna Haaland

A Poet's Curse by Michael Estabrook

My Life in Cars by Linda Strever

A Democracy Divided by Ralph J. Long Jr.

Fireweed by Gudrun Bortman

and more . . .